To Krista,

Happy 18th Birthday

Love, Grandma ♡

Angels Watching Over You

LOVE · PEACE · JOY · Speak Kind Words · Kindness · Believe · Patience · Hope · There is No Fear in Love

Carol Endres

CAROL J. ENDRES

HARVEST HOUSE PUBLISHERS
Eugene, Oregon

For he will command
his angels concerning you to
guard you in all your ways.

THE BOOK OF PSALMS

Let there be Peace in the Country

Blessings

All the blessings we enjoy are Divine deposits, committed to our trust on this condition, that they should be dispensed for the benefit of our neighbors.

JOHN CALVIN

Praise

4

Every good and perfect gift is from above, coming down from the Father of the heavenly lights...

THE BOOK OF JAMES

Reflect upon your present blessings, of which every man has many; not on your past misfortunes, of which all men have some.

CHARLES DICKENS

The blessed and inviting truth is that God is the most winsome of all beings and in our worship of Him we should find unspeakable pleasure.

A. W. TOZER

All praise to Thee, my God, this night,
For all the blessings of the light!
Keep me, O keep me, King of kings,
Beneath Thine own almighty wings

THOMAS KEN

God from whom all blessings flow!

THOMAS KEN

5

Love is a fruit in season at all times

Love is a great beautifier.

LOUISA MAY ALCOTT

If I planted a flower every time I thought of you, I could walk in my garden forever.

AUTHOR UNKNOWN

Make yourself familiar with the angels... for without being seen, they are present with you.

ST. FRANCIS DE SALES

God loves each of us as if there were only one of us.

SAINT AUGUSTINE

Love cultivates love...

nd within the reach of every hand.

MOTHER TERESA

A weed is no more than a flower in disguise.

JAMES RUSSELL LOWELL

He who sows courtesy reaps friendship, and he who plants kindness gathers love.

SAINT BASIL

At cool of day, with God I walk
My garden's grateful shade;
I hear His voice among the trees
And I am not afraid.

AUTHOR UNKNOWN

Flowers are the alphabet of angels, whereby they write on the hills and fields mysterious truths.

BENJAMIN FRANKLIN

Pull weeds of selfishness and love will bloom.

CAROL ENDRES

Spring bursts today,
For Christ is risen and all the earth's at play.
...Sing, creatures, sing,
Angels and men and birds, and everything...

CHRISTINA G. ROSSETTI

Blessed is the nation

America is the crucible of God. It is the melting pot where all races are fusing and reforming...these are the fires of God you've come to... into the crucible with you all. God is making the American.

ISRAEL ZANGWELL
The Melting Pot

Patriotism consists not in waving the flag, but in striving that our country shall be righteous as well as strong.

JAMES BRYCE

whose God is the Lord.

THE BOOK OF PSALMS

God's angels are about the nation, opening our hearts to His grace.

CAROL ENDRES

America! America!
God shed His grace on thee...

KATHERINE LEE BATES

Around our pillows golden ladders rise,
And up and down the skies,
With winged sandals shod,
The angels come, and go, the Messengers of God!

RICHARD HENRY STODDARD

Righteousness exalts a nation.

THE BOOK OF PROVERBS

My country, 'tis of thee,
Sweet land of liberty,
Of thee I sing;
Land where my fathers died,
Land of the pilgrims' pride,
From ev'ry mountain-side
Let freedom ring!

SAMUEL F. SMITH

Stone walls do not a prison make,
Nor iron bars a cage;
Minds innocent and quiet take
That for an hermitage;
If I have freedom in my love,
And in my soul am free,
Angels alone that soar above
Enjoy such liberty.

RICHARD LOVELACE

We the people of the United States, in order to form a more perfect union, establish justice, insure domestic tranquility, provide for the common defense, promote the general welfare, and secure the blessings of liberty to ourselves and our posterity, do ordain and establish this Constitution for the United States of America.

THE U.S. CONSTITUTION

Proclaim liberty throughout

12

the land to all its inhabitants!

God Creates Angels To Be
Sparkling and Unique, Just Like
Snowflakes Each One Different
Carol Endres ©

The splendor of Silence,—of snow-jeweled hills and of ice.

INGRAM CROCKETT

For by him all things were created: things in heaven and on earth, visible and invisible...

THE BOOK OF COLOSSIANS

Like snowflakes, the human pattern is never cast twice. We are uncommonly and marvelously intricate in thought and action, our problems are most complex and, too often, silently borne.

ALICE CHILDRESS

Whenever a snowflake leaves the sky,
It turns and turns to say "Good-by!
Good-by, dear clouds, so cool and gray!"
Then lightly travels on its way.

MARY MAPES DODGE

In this dim world of clouding cares,
We rarely know, till wildered eyes
See white wings lessening up the skies,
The angels with us unawares.

GERALD MASSEY

The helmed Cherubim,
And sworded Seraphim,
Are seen in glittering ranks with wings display'd.

JOHN MILTON

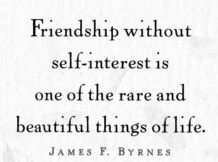

All love that has not friendship for its base,
Is like a mansion built upon the sand.

ELLA WHEELER WILCOX

Friendship without
self-interest is
one of the rare and
beautiful things of life.

JAMES F. BYRNES

I believe that
unarmed truth and
unconditional love
will have the final
word in reality.
That is why
right, temporarily
defeated, is
stronger than
evil triumphant.

MARTIN LUTHER KING, JR.

A friend is a person with whom I may be sincere. Before him I may think aloud.

RALPH WALDO EMERSON

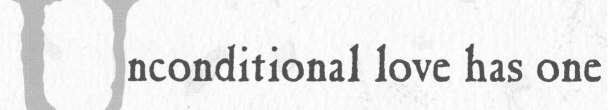

Unconditional love has one

condition—no selfishness allowed.

CAROL ENDRES

17

LOVE * KEEPS * THE WORLD
TURNING THRU THE
AGES

CAROL ENDRES

Look round our world; behold the chain of love
Combining all below and all above.

ALEXANDER POPE

Angels represent the Father's heart
of love throughout the universe.

CAROL ENDRES

The angels are the
dispensers and
administrators of the
Divine beneficence
toward us; they regard
our safety, undertake
our defense, direct our
ways, and exercise a
constant solicitude
that no evil befall us.

JOHN CALVIN

*Our way lies where God knows
And Love knows where:
We are in Love's hand today.*

ALGERNON CHARLES SWINBURNE

To love is to believe, to hope, to know;
'Tis an essay, a taste of heaven below!

EDMUND WALLER

The morning stars sang together

Hark! the herald angels sing,
"Glory to the newborn King;
Peace on earth, and mercy mild;
God and sinners reconciled."

CHARLES WESLEY

O for a
thousand
tongues to sing
my great
Redeemer's
praise!

CHARLES WESLEY

Music is well said to be the speech of angels.

THOMAS CARLYLE

I believe angels
sing songs of
praise to God
along with us.

CAROL ENDRES

As we offer our small rejoicing
For the love that surrounds our days,
All the wonderful works of Thy goodness
Shall open before our gaze;
Through the gates of our narrow thanksgiving
We shall enter Thy courts of praise.

ANNIE JOHNSON FLINT

And flights of angels sing thee to thy rest!

WILLIAM SHAKESPEARE

and all the angels shouted for joy...

LOVE JOY PEACE

ANGELS

Angels tread here on earth,

The angel of the Lord encamps around those who fear him, and he delivers them.

THE BOOK OF PSALMS

For lo! the days are hastening on,
By prophet-bards foretold,
When with the ever-circling years,
Comes round the age of gold;
When Peace shall over all the earth
Its ancient splendors fling
And the whole world send back the song
Which now the angels sing.

EDMUND HAMILTON SEARS

Angels are ever all around us
And with His love, they do surround us.
When my heart is sore in need
The angels come, my soul to feed.
They come to me from up above,
And sing in whispers of His love.
When in my heart I feel a tug
I know that it's an angel's hug.

PAUL DAMMANN

In almost everything that touches our everyday life on earth, God is pleased when we're pleased. He wills that we be as free as birds to soar and sing our maker's praise without anxiety.

A. W. TOZER

bringing God's love, joy, and peace.

CAROL ENDRES

Praise the Lord, you his angels, you mighty ones who do his bidding, who obey his word.

Praise the Lord, all his heavenly hosts, you his servants who do his will.

THE BOOK OF PSALMS

Angels are God's messengers.

Angels are spiritual beings created by God to serve Him. They are very powerful beings who function as God's messengers.

PAT ROBERTSON

God doesn't send them because we deserve it. He sends them because we need help. Angels are literally messengers of God's mercy.

MAC HAMMOND

*They come, God's messengers of love,
they come from realms of peace above,
from homes of never-fading light,
from blissful mansions ever bright.*

*They come to watch around us here,
to soothe our sorrow, calm our fear:
ye heavenly guides, speed not away,
God willeth you with us to stay.*

ROBERT CAMPBELL
"God's Messengers of Love"

Are not all angels ministering spirits sen

to serve those who will inherit salvation?

THE BOOK OF HEBREWS

ANGEL OF HEARTS

LOVE IS FOREVER

Carol Cardoza

None but God can satisfy the longings of an immortal soul; that as the heart was made for Him, so He only can fill it.

RICHARD
CHENEVIX TRENCH

Angels

For where your treasure is, there your heart will be also.

THE BOOK OF LUKE

There is a place of comfort sweet,
Near to the heart of God.
A place where we our Savior meet,
Near to the heart of God.

O Jesus, blest Redeemer,
Sent from the heart of God,
Hold us who wait before Thee
Near to the heart of God.

There is a place of full release,
Near to the heart of God.
A place where all is joy and peace,
Near to the heart of God.

CLELAND B. MCAFEE
"Near to the Heart of God"

God has two dwellings:
one in heaven, and the other
in a meek and thankful heart.

IZAAK WALTON

bring us the very heart of God.

CAROL ENDRES

27

Angels remind us of all we can "bee" in and with God's love.

CAROL ENDRES

The reason why we can hope to find God is that He is here, engaged all the time in finding us. Every pulse of love is a tendril that draws us in His direction.

RUFUS JONES

Love is not a possession but a growth. The heart is a lamp with just oil enough to burn for an hour, and if there be no oil to put in again its light will go out. God's grace is the oil that fills the lamp of love.

HENRY WARD BEECHER

Riches take wings, comforts vanish, away, but love stays with us.

Your worst days are never so bad that you are beyond the reach of God's grace. And your best days are never so good that you are beyond the need of God's grace.

JERRY BRIDGES

hope withers
God is love.

LEW WALLACE

BEE WISE · BEE HAVE

BEE JOYFUL · BEE KIND · BEE SHY

BEE HAPPY · BEELIEVE · BEE WARE

BEE GOOD · BEE MINE

BEE HAVEN

POLLEN

Queen Bee

Whatever we are waiting for—peace of mind, contentment, grace, the inner awareness of simple abundance—it will surely come to us, but only when we are ready to receive it with an open and grateful heart.

SARAH BAN
BREATHNACH

Lord make me an instrument of your peace.

—St. Francis of Assisi

Peace is not the absence of conflict from life, but the ability to cope with it.

ANONYMOUS

Be good, keep your feet dry, your eyes open, your heart at peace, and your soul in the joy of Christ.

THOMAS MERTON

Like a river glorious is God's perfect peace,
Over all victorious in its bright increase;
Perfect, yet it floweth fuller everyday;
Perfect, yet it groweth deeper all the way.

Stayed upon Jehovah, hearts are fully blest;
Finding, as He promised, perfect peace and rest.

FRANCES R. HAVERGAL

Where there is peace, God is.

GEORGE HERBERT

Rocked in the cradle of the deep
I lay me down in peace to sleep;
Secure I rest upon the wave,
For Thou, O Lord! hast power to save.

EMMA HART WILLARD

31

I sowed the seeds of love, it was all in the spring,
In April, May, and June, likewise, when small birds they do sing;
My garden's well planted with flowers everywhere,
Yet I had not the liberty to choose for myself the flower that I loved so dear.

MRS. FLEETWOOD HABERGAM

Friendship is love with understanding.

OLD PROVERB

You will find as you look back upon your life that the moments when you have really lived are the moments when you have done things in the spirit of love.

HENRY DRUMMOND

Kindness is the golden key that unlocks the hearts of others.

AUTHOR UNKNOWN

Love is patient, love is kind ... It always protects, always trusts, always hopes, always perseveres.

THE BOOK OF 1 CORINTHIANS

LOVE IS KIND

BIRD Whistles

SEED

Let your dreams soar to the sky!

For with faith and trust in God, no goal can be too high.

34

O welcome pure-eyed Faith, white-handed Hope,

Thou hovering angel, girt with golden wings!

JOHN MILTON

We need time to dream, time to remember, and time to reach the infinite. Time to be.

GLADYS TABER

O passing Angel, speed me with a song,

A melody of heaven to reach my heart

And rouse me to the race and make me strong.

CHRISTINA ROSSETTI

To accomplish great things, we must dream as well as act.

ANATOLE FRANCE

For you are with me; your your staff, they comfort

The Book of Psalms

You may call God love, you may call God goodness. But the best name for God is compassion.

MEISTER ECKHART

When you are in the dark, listen, and God will give you a very precious message for someone else when you get into the light.

OSWALD CHAMBERS

Praise the LORD, O my soul, and forget not all his benefits— who forgives all your sins and heals all your diseases, who redeems your life from the pit and crowns you with love and compassion, who satisfies your desires with good things so that your youth is renewed like the eagle's.

THE BOOK OF PSALMS

May your unfailing love be my comfort, according to your promise to your servant. Let your compassion come to me that I may live.

THE BOOK OF PSALMS

rod and
me.

God stirs up our comfortable nests, and pushes us over the edge of them, and we are forced to use our wings to save ourselves from fatal falling. Read your trials in this light, and see if your wings are being developed.

HANNAH
WHITALL SMITH

Praise be to
the Father of Compassion

Who comforts us in all
our troubles. —2 Corinthians 1:3-4

Love accepts the trying things of
life without asking for explanations.
It trusts and is at rest.

AMY CARMICHAEL

Be glad of life
because it gives
you the chance
to love, to
work, to play,
and to look up
at the stars.

HENRY VAN DYKE

Love never fails.

THE BOOK OF 1 CORINTHIANS

Seasons change, friends move away, and life goes on from day to day.
Flowers fade and streams go dry and many times we wonder why.
Yet we can always be assured because God tells us in His Word,
That unlike changes in the weather, love goes on and lasts forever!

AUTHOR UNKNOWN

It is not how much
we have, but how
much we enjoy, that
makes happiness.

CHARLES SPURGEON

Somehow the Angels comfort me whenever I have tears,
And always they encourage me to overcome my fears.
I tell them all of my troubles when they seem too much to bear,
And I put my faith and confidence in their almighty care.

MARTINA TARANDEK

Sleep, my child, and peace attend thee
All through the night.
Guardian angels God will send thee,
All through the night.

SIR HAROLD BOULTON

All night, all day,
Angels watching over me, my Lord.
All night, all day,
Angels watching over me.

NEGRO SPIRITUAL

The guardian angels of life sometimes fly so high as to be beyond our sight, but they are always looking down upon us.

JEAN PAUL RICHTER

God always has an angel of help fo

Angels watch over us

those who are willing to do their duty.

T. L. CUYLER

41

We may run, walk, stumble, drive, or fly, but let us never lose sight o

We know that all things work together for good to those who love God . . .

THE BOOK OF ROMANS (NKJV)

And God said,"...I have set my rainbow in the clouds, and it will be the sign of the covenant between me and the earth. Whenever I bring clouds over the earth and the rainbow appears in the clouds, I will remember my covenant between me and you and all living creatures of every kind. Never again will the waters become a flood to destroy all life. Whenever the rainbow appears in the clouds, I will see it and remember the everlasting covenant between God and all living creatures of every kind on the earth."

THE BOOK OF GENESIS

Ah, great it is to believe the dream as we
stand in youth by the starry stream;
but a greater thing is to fight life through
and say at the end, the dream is true!

EDWIN MARKHAM

May the sun always shine on your windowpane;
May a rainbow be certain to follow each rain;
May the hand of a friend always be near you;
May God fill your heart with gladness to cheer you.

IRISH BLESSING

the reason for the journey, or miss a chance to see a rainbow on the way.

GLORIA GAITHER

43

I went forth to find an angel
And found this effort brought
That life is full of so much good
The touch that angels wrought.

JAMES JOSEPH HUESGEN

But we can all be angels to one another. We can choose to obey the still small stirring within, the little whisper that says, "Go. Ask. Reach out. Be an answer to someone's plea. You have a part to play. Have faith."…The world will be a better place for it. And wherever they are, the angels will dance.

JOAN WESTER ANDERSON

"We must join hands—so," said Anne gravely. "It ought to be over running water. We'll just imagine this path is running water. I'll repeat the oath first. I solemnly swear to be faithful to my bosom friend, Diana Barry, as long as the sun and moon shall endure. Now you say it and put my name in."

Diana repeated the "oath" with a laugh fore and aft. Then she said:

"You're a queer girl, Anne. I heard before that you were queer. But I believe I'm going to like you real well."

L. M. MONTGOMERY
Anne of Green Gables

Angels are inseparable friends, who bring strength and consolation to those who include them in their lives. In truth, angels are our best friends.

JANICE T. CONNELL

LOVE IS PATIENT I COR.13:4

FROM YOUR FRIEND

45

HEAVENLY

RAIN

SHOWERS

CAROL ENDRES

46

How blessings brighten as they take their flight!

EDWARD YOUNG

The Lord who is "rich in mercy" not only forgives sins but also chooses the soul to dwell in His presence. The soul opens itself to those lights, graces, and blessings that shower on it new strength as the gentle dew. It is the abundance of these gifts that lift the soul to enjoy the favors of the Lord.

AUTHOR UNKNOWN

There shall be showers of blessing:
This is the promise of love;
There shall be seasons refreshing,
Sent from the Savior above.

Showers of blessing,
Showers of blessing we need:
Mercy drops round us are falling,
But for the showers we plead.

DANIEL W. WHITTLE

Hush, my dear, lie still and slumber!
Holy angels guard thy bed!
Heavenly blessings without number
Gently falling on thy head.

ISAAC WATTS

47

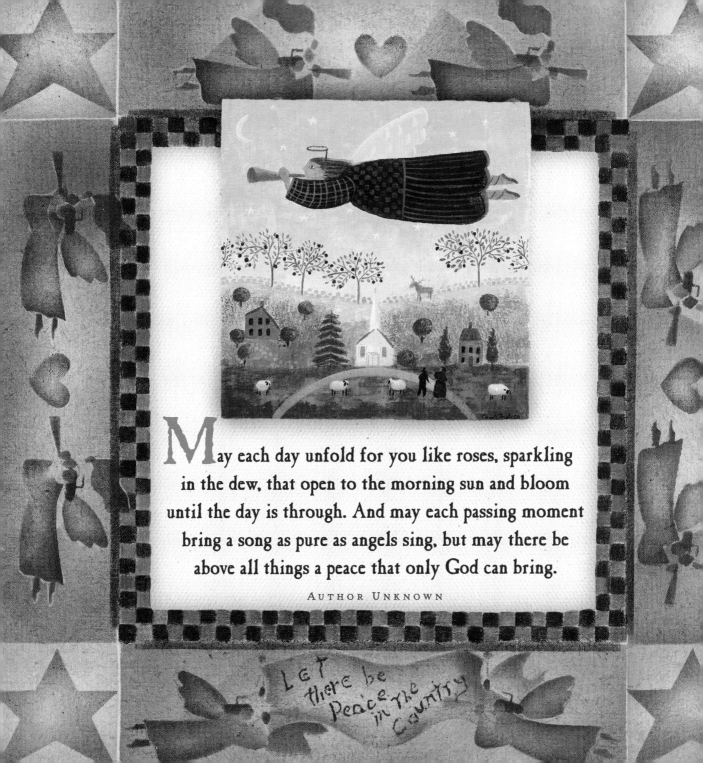

May each day unfold for you like roses, sparkling
in the dew, that open to the morning sun and bloom
until the day is through. And may each passing moment
bring a song as pure as angels sing, but may there be
above all things a peace that only God can bring.

AUTHOR UNKNOWN

Let there be Peace in the Country